# TopicFinder

to accompany

# THE ART OF PUBLIC SPEAKING
### Ninth Edition

## STEPHEN E. LUCAS
*University of Wisconsin—Madison*

Boston   Burr Ridge, IL   Dubuque, IA   Madison, WI   New York   San Francisco   St. Louis
Bangkok   Bogotá   Caracas   Kuala Lumpur   Lisbon   London   Madrid   Mexico City
Milan   Montreal   New Delhi   Santiago   Seoul   Singapore   Sydney   Taipei   Toronto

The McGraw·Hill Companies

# McGraw-Hill Higher Education

TopicFinder for use with
THE ART OF PUBLIC SPEAKING
Stephen E. Lucas

1 2 3 4 5 6 7 8 9 0 DOC/DOC 0 9 8 7 6 5

ISBN-13: 978-0-07-321646-1
ISBN-10:     0-07-321646-1

www.mhhe.com

## INTRODUCTION

Choosing a topic is the first step in preparing a successful speech. In Chapter 4 of *The Art of Public Speaking*, you will read about several methods you can use to select an interesting and appropriate topic. The purpose of this booklet is to provide additional help by identifying more than 1,200 topics from A to Z.

As you read this booklet, keep in mind that there is no limit to the number of potential speech topics. Those listed here are meant to stimulate your creativity, not to limit it. Some of the topics are very broad (economics, South America, mass transportation). Others are more specific (value-added tax, Amazon River, airplane safety). Some are suitable for informative speeches; others for persuasive speeches. Many will work for either kind of speech, depending on how you approach the topic and develop your ideas.

Whatever topic you choose, remember it is only the first step in preparing your speech. As explained in Chapter 4 of the textbook, once you have a topic, you will then need to narrow it and come up with a sharp, clear specific purpose that you can achieve in the time allotted for your speech. You also will need to research the speech, prepare a detailed outline of it, and practice your delivery. The sooner you choose a topic, the more time you will have for the rest of your speech preparation. I hope you will find this booklet a valuable resource that will help you get started on the right foot.

Stephen E. Lucas

## A

abolitionism
Academy Awards
accordions
acting
acupuncture
Addams, Jane
adoption laws
adventure travel
advertising
aerobics
Aesop's Fables
affirmative action
African history
Afrocentrism
age discrimination
AIDS
airplane safety
Alamo
alcoholism
algae
allergies
alternate energy
Amazon River
ambulances
Amish
Amnesty International
Amtrak
anarchism
anemia
anesthesia

Angelou, Maya
anger management
animal rights
Anthony, Susan B.
antibacterial products
antiques
anxiety
Appalachian Trail
Apple Computer
aquariums
Aquinas, St. Thomas
archaeology
architecture
Armstrong, Lance
aromatherapy
arson
art
arthrosporic surgery
artificial intelligence
aspirin
asteroids
asthma
astronomy
atomic fusion
attention deficit
    disorder
aurora borealis
Austen, Jane
Australia
auto racing
avian flu
Aztecs

## B

Babylon
back pain
badlands
bagpipes
Balkans
ballet
ballroom dancing
bankruptcy
Barton, Clara
baseball
Bastille Day
batik
Bay of Pigs
beaches
Beatles
beavers
bees
Bell, Alexander
    Graham
Beowulf
Berlin Wall
Bethune, Mary
    McLeod
Better Business Bureau
bicycles
bigfoot
bilingual education
Bill of Rights
billiards
Bin Laden, Osama
biodiversity

1

biography
biometrics
bird watching
birth order
birthmarks
black holes
Blackbeard
blindness
blood types
bluegrass music
boating safety
bocci
body language
Boer War
Bolívar, Simón
Bombay
bone diseases
boomerangs
bottled water
bowling
boxing
braiding
braille
brain
breast cancer
Broadway musicals
Brontë, Emily
Buddhism
buffalo
bullfighting
butterflies

# C
calligraphy
Cambodia
campaign finance
camping
campus safety
Canada
Cannes Film Festival
canoeing
card games
carpentry
cartography
cartoons
Cassatt, Mary
catacombs
cats
censorship
census
Chavez, Cesar
cheese
chess
chewing tobacco
child abuse
child custody laws
Chinese New Year
chiropractic
chocolate
church-state relations
Cinco de Mayo
civil rights
Civil War

classic films
Cleopatra
climate
clocks
cloning
clouds
coaching
coastal erosion
cockroaches
coffee
Cold War
college athletics
comets
community service
computer viruses
Confucius
consumer rights
cooking
coral reefs
counterfeiting
court system
cowboys
Crazy Horse
crime prevention
crossword puzzles
Crusades
cryptology
Cuba
cults
cybernetics
cystic fibrosis

# D

D-Day
dairy farming
Dalai Lama
dams
darts
date rape
daydreams
daylight-saving time
Dead Sea scrolls
deafness
death penalty
Death Valley
decaying bridges
deer
deism
dementia
democracy
demography
Denmark
dentistry
depression
detectives
Día de los muertos
diabetes
diamonds
Dickens, Charles
Dickinson, Emily
dictators
digital divide
diets

diplomacy
disability laws
Disneyland
distributed computing
diversity
diving
divorce
Dix, Dorothea
DNA fingerrint
documentaries
dog racing
domestic violence
Dominican Republic
Douglass, Frederick
doulas
Down syndrome
Dr. Seuss
Dracula
dragons
dream catchers
drug laws
druids
drunken driving
DuBois, W.E.B.
dust mites
Dylan, Bob
dynamite
dyslexia

# E

E. coli bacteria
e-commerce

eagles
Earhart, Amelia
earthquakes
Easter Island
eating disorders
Ebola virus
eclipses
eco-terrorism
ecology
economics
ecstasy
edible flowers
Edison, Thomas
education reform
eels
egalitarianism
Eiffel Tower
Einstein, Albert
El Salvador
elderly drivers
Electoral College
electric cars
electroshock therapy
elephants
Ellis Island
Emancipation
  Proclamation
emergency rooms
emotions
Empire State Building
encyclopedias
endangered species

energy shortages
engineering
English-only laws
entertainment law
environment
Epicureans
epidemics
epilepsy
Epstein-Barr virus
equestrian contests
ergonomics
Erie Canal
Eskimos
espionage
ethics
Ethiopia
etiquette
eugenics
euthanasia
evangelism
Everglades
evolution
exercise
existentialism
extrasensory
  perception
extraterrestrial
  intelligence
eyewitness testimony

**F**
Fabergé

fables
falcons
families
famine
farming
fascism
fast food
fatherhood
feminism
fencing
Feng Shui
ferrets
fertility drugs
feudalism
figure skating
Fiji Islands
film editing
financial planning
fingerprints
fire ants
fire prevention
fireworks
first aid
First Amendment
Fitzgerald, Ella
flags
flamenco
flat tax
fleas
flightless birds
floods
fluoride

flutes
fly fishing
fog
folklore
food safety
football
foreign aid
forensic medicine
forestry
forgery
Fort Knox
fossils
foster care
Four-H
free trade
French cuisine
Freud, Sigmund
friendship
frogs
frostbite
fugitives
funding for the arts
fungus
furniture

**G**
Galápagos Islands
Galileo
gambling
Gandhi, Mahatma
gangsters
Garden of Eden

gardening

garlic

garment industry

Garvey, Marcus

gasoline

gastroenterology

gay rights

geisha

gemstones

genealogy

genetic engineering

geodesic domes

geology

germ warfare

Geronimo

Gershwin, George

Gestalt therapy

Gettysburg

Ghana

ghosts

giant redwoods

gift-giving

ginseng

glaciers

gladiators

Glasgow

glass

global warming

globalization

gold

Golden Gate Bridge

Goldman, Emma

golf

grading systems

graffiti

Grand Canyon

grandparents

grasshoppers

Grave's disease

Great Barrier Reef

Greek Orthodox
  Church

Greenpeace

Greenwich Village

greeting cards

greyhounds

grief

grizzly bears

Guantánamo Bay

Guinea

guitars

gun control

gymnastics

## H

Habitat for Humanity

Hadrian's Wall

haiku

Halley's comet

Halloween

handwriting

Harlem

harmonicas

Hawaii

hawks

headaches

health laboratories

hearing loss

heart disease

hepatitis

herbs

heroes

heroin

Hiawatha

hibernation

hieroglyphics

hiking

Hindenburg

Hinduism

hip hop

Hiroshima

Hispanic culture

Hmong

Hodgkin's disease

Holiday, Billie

holistic medicine

Holland

Holmes, Sherlock

Holocaust

home schooling

homelessness

homeopathy

homesteading

Hong Kong

Hope diamond

horticulture

hormone therapy
horror movies
horse racing
hospice
hot dogs
hot air balloons
Houdini
Huerta, Delores
Humane Society
humor
hunger
hurricanes
hybrid cars
hypnosis
hypothermia

# I

Ice Age
icebergs
Iceland
identity theft
iguanas
illiteracy
immigration
immune system
impeachment
imperialism
impressionism
Inca
incense
incivility
income tax

Independence Day
India
Indianapolis 500
indigo
individualism
industrial revolution
infant mortality
infertility
inflation
influence peddling
influenza
ink
inoculations
insanity defense
insects
insomnia
Istanbul
insurance fraud
intellectual property
intelligent design
   theory
interest groups
interest rates
interior design
Internal Revenue
   Service
International Bank
internships
introspection
inventions
invertebrates
IQ tests

Iraq
iron
Iroquois
irradiation
irrigation
Islam
isometric exercise
Israel
Istanbul
ivory
Iwo Jima

# J

Jack the Ripper
jack-o'-lanterns
Jackson, Mahalia
jade
jaguars
jai lai
jailbreaks
Jainism
Jakarta
jalapeños
jambalaya
Jamestown
Japanese lanterns
jargon
jasmine
Java
jaw disorders
jazz
jeans

jeeps

Jefferson, Thomas

Jekyll and Hyde

jellyfish

Jerusalem

jesters

jet lag

jet skis

jet stream

jewelry

jigsaw puzzles

Jihad

Jim Crow laws

jitterbug

Joan of Arc

job hunting

Johannesburg

Joint Chiefs of Staff

jokes

Joplin, Scott

Jordan, Barbara

journalism

Judaism

judicial reform

juggling

juicing

jujitsu

jukeboxes

Juneteenth

Jungian psychology

jungles

juniper trees

junk bonds

Jupiter

Jurassic Period

jurisprudence

jury trials

# K

Kabuki

Kafka, Franz

Kahlo, Frida

Kalahari Desert

kaleidoscopes

kangaroos

karaoke

karate

Kashmir

kava

kayaking

kazoos

Keller, Helen

Kelley, Abigail

kelp

kendo

Kennedy, John F.

kennels

Kentucky Derby

Kenya

ketchup

Key West

keys

kibbutz

kickboxing

kidnaping

Killarney

killer whales

kimonos

kindergarten

kinesiology

kinetic art

King Kong

King, Billie Jean

King Charles spaniel

kinship

Kirlian photography

kitchens

kites

Kitty Hawk

kleptomania

Klondike

knees

Knesset

knights

knitting

knives

Knossos

koala bears

Kon Tiki

Koran

Korean War

kosher food

Ku Klux Klan

Kwanza

Khmer Rouge

## L

Labor Day
Labrador retrievers
lace
lacrosse
ladybugs
lakes
land use policies
land mines
landfills
landscape architecture
landslides
Lange, Dorothea
language
Laos
laser surgery
Las Vegas
latex allergies
laughter
lava
Lawrence of Arabia
lead poisoning
League of Women Voters
learning disabilities
Lee, Bruce
leeches
leopards
Leopold and Loeb
leprechauns
leprosy
letter writing

levitation
Lewis and Clark
libertarians
Liberty Bell
libraries
lice
lichen
light therapy
lighthouses
lightning
Liliuokalani
limestone
limnology
limousines
linguistics
liposuction
liquor laws
listening
literacy
llamas
lobsters
Loch Ness monster
logging
Louisiana Purchase
Louvre Museum
low-income housing
lullabies
lutes
lymphoma
lynching

## M

Madrid
mafia
Magna Carta
magnet schools
mahjong
mail-order fraud
malaria
Malcolm X
managed care
management styles
manatees
Mandela, Nelson
Mankiller, Wilma
maps
marathons
Mardi Gras
Marines
marriage customs
Mars
martial arts
Masai carving
masks
mass transportation
massage
Mead, Margaret
media violence
medical privacy rules
meditation
Mennonites
mercury

Mesa Verde
meteorology
Middle Ages
migrant workers
milk
minimum wage
mining
modernism
mold
monarch butterflies
moon
Mormonism
Morrison, Toni
Morse code
Mother's Day
moths
motorcycles
Mount Kilimanjaro
mountain climbing
movie-rating system
Muhammad
multiple sclerosis
mummies
mushrooms
music therapy
mythology

**N**
NAACP
nannies
Napoleon
napping

NASCAR
national defense
national health care
national debt
national parks
National Football
  League
Native Americans
natural foods
naturalization
naturopathy
Navajo
Naval Academy
Nazism
near-death experiences
needlepoint
negotiation strategy
neonatal care
Nepal
neuroses
New Age religions
New Zealand
New York Stock
  Exchange
newspapers
Newton, Isaac
Nez Perce
Niagara Falls
nicotine
Nielsen ratings
night blindness
nightmares

nihilism
Nile River
Noah's ark
Nobel Prize
nocturnal mammals
noise pollution
nomads
nonfat foods
North Korea
North Pole
Nostradamus
nuclear power
nuclear proliferation
numerology
numismatics
nurse shortages
nursery rhymes
nursing homes
nutrition
nylon

**O**
oats
Obama, Barak
obesity
obscenity
occultism
occupational therapy
oceanography
octopus
Odyssey
O'Keefe, Georgia

Oktoberfest
olive oil
Olympic games
Ontario
opals
open classrooms
open records laws
open-source software
opera
opinion polls
opium
optical illusions
optimism
optometry
oral cultures
orangutans
orchards
orchids
Oregon Trail
organ donation
organic agriculture
organized labor
Oriental rugs
origami
ornithology
orphanages
orthodontics
orthopedics
Orwell, George
Oslo
osteoporosis
ostriches

Ottawa
otters
Ottoman Empire
Ouija boards
out-of-body experiences
outdoor education
ovarian cancer
Owens, Jesse
owls
oysters
Ozark Mountains

## P

Pacific Ocean
painless dentistry
paintball
paleontology
Palestine
palm reading
Panama Canal
pandas
panic attacks
pantomime
parachuting
parades
parasites
parenting
Parliament
Passover
patents
patriotism

Peace Corps
peanuts
Pearl Harbor
personal finance
Peru
pesticides
pets
Pharaohs
pharmaceuticals
phishing scams
phobias
photography
physical therapy
Picasso, Pablo
pilates
pirates
plastic surgery
Pocahontas
poetry
pointillism
poker
polar bears
porcelain
pornography
postage stamps
pottery
poverty
prayer in schools
prescription drugs
presidency
Presley, Elvis
price fixing

prison industry

privacy laws

product recalls

prostate cancer

prostitution

psychical research

public broadcasting

Puerto Rico

Pulitzer Prize

## Q

quackery

Quakerism

quality control

quarries

quarterbacks

Quebec

Queen Elizabeth

quicksand

quilting

quintuplets

quiz shows

quotas

## R

rabies

raccoons

racial profiling

radiation therapy

Radio City Music Hall

ragtime

railroads

rain forest

Ramadan

rats

real estate

reality television

recycling

Red Cross

Red Sea

reflexology

refugees

regattas

reggae

reincarnation

reindeer

relaxation techniques

religious schools

reproductive rights

reptiles

rescue methods

restaurants

resumé writing

retirement plans

revolutions

riboflavin

rice

risk management

Robeson, Paul

robots

rock climbing

rodeos

roller coasters

Roosevelt, Eleanor

roses

Rosetta stone

Rosh Hashanah

ROTC

rowing

rugby

## S

sailing

Salem witch trials

salmon

salt

Santa Claus

Saudi Arabia

schizophrenia

school bus safety

school choice

scorpions

Scotland

Scrabble

seaweed

Secret Service

self-defense

September 11

sewing

sexual harassment

Shakespeare, William

Shanghai

sharks

shoplifting

siblings

sickle-cell anemia

Sikhism
silent movies
Sistine Chapel
skiing
skydiving
slam poetry
sleep deprivation
Smithsonian Institute
smokeless tobacco
snow
soccer
Social Security
socialism
softball
South America
space exploration
Spain
Special Olympics
speech codes
speed limits
spiders
spies
Splenda
St. John's Wort
standardized testing
stem-cell research
steroids
stock market
story telling
stress
student loans
student rights

study abroad
subways
suffrage
sugar
suicide
support groups
surfing
sushi
sweatshops
swing music

# T

table tennis
tae kwon do
Taj Mahal
talk shows
Talmud
tanning salons
tap dancing
tarantulas
tarot
tattoos
taxes
taxicabs
taxidermy
tea
teacher certification
Tecumseh
teenage drivers
telekinesis
telemarketing
television news

tenants' rights
tennis
terrorism
testosterone
Thanksgiving
thermodynamics
Thucydides
thunderstorms
Tibet
Tiffany glass
tires
Titanic
Title IX
tobacco
tofu
topiary
tornadoes
totems
Tour de France
Tourette's syndrome
tourism
Tower of London
Trail of Tears
transcendentalism
troglodytes
trolley cars
truth in advertising
tsetse fly
tsunamis
tuberculosis
Tubman, Harriet
tuition

tulips

twins

typhoid fever

typhoons

**U**

UFOs

ukuleles

ulcers

ultraviolet radiation

Ulysses

umbrellas

Uncle Sam

Underground Railroad

undersea life

unemployment

UNICEF

unicorns

unilateralism

Unitarianism

United Nations

United States Mint

uranium

urban planning

Uruguay

utilitarianism

**V**

vacations

vaccines

vacuum cleaners

value-added tax

vampire bats

van Gogh, Vincent

vandalism

vanilla

Vatican

vaudeville

veganism

Venice

ventriloquism

venture capitalism

Vermeer, Johannes

vertigo

Vesuvius

veterinarians

victims' rights

video games

vikings

vinegar

violins

Virgin Islands

viruses

vitamins

viticulture

voiceprints

VoIP

volcanoes

volleyball

volunteering

voodoo

voting reform

**W**

wage scales

Wailing Wall

wallpapering

walruses

war crimes

Warhol, Andy

Washington, D.C.

waste management

watchdogs

water ballet

water shortages

water safety

water polo

water skiing

waterfalls

watermelon

wax museums

weather forecasting

weaving

weblogs

weddings

weightlifting

welfare

Wells, Ida B.

werewolves

West Nile Virus

West Bank

wetlands

whales

whirling dervishes

White House
white-water rafting
whooping cranes
Wiesel, Elie
wildebeest
wilderness
Wimbledon
wind power
wind surfing
wine
winter
wisdom teeth
wit
witchcraft
Wollstonecraft, Mary
wolves
women's rights
woodworking
wool
word games
workers' rights
World Trade
  Organization
World War II
worms
Wounded Knee
wrestling
Wright, Frank Lloyd

# X

x-rays
Xavier, Frances

xenophobia
Xenophon
xerography
xylography
xylophones
XYZ affair

# Y

y chromosome
yachts
Yahtzee
Yalta Conference
yams
Yangtze River
Yankee Doodle
yard sales
yellow fever
yellow journalism
Yellowstone
Yemen
yeti
yin and yang
YMCA
yodeling
yoga
yogurt
Yom Kippur
Yosemite
Young, Brigham
youth sports
Yucàtan peninsula
yucca

Yugoslavia
Yukon Territory

# Z

Zaire
Zapata, Emiliano
zebra mussels
Zen
zeppelins
Zeus
Ziegfeld Follies
Zimbabwe
zinc
Zionism
zip codes
zippers
zithers
zodiac
zombies
zoning laws
zoology
zoos
Zoroastrianism
Zorro
Zulu
Zuni
zydeco

# Notes

# Notes

# Notes

# Notes

# Notes

# Notes